THE TRENCH

OLIVER LANSLEY

THE TRENCH

OBERON BOOKS
LONDON

WWW.OBERONBOOKS.COM

First published in 2012 by Oberon Books Ltd
521 Caledonian Road, London N7 9RH
Tel: +44 (0) 20 7607 3637 / Fax: +44 (0) 20 7607 3629
e-mail: info@oberonbooks.com
www.oberonbooks.com

A catalogue record for this book is available from the British Library.

PB ISBN: 978-1-84943-453-9
Digital ISBN: 978-1-84943-540-6

Cover and book images by Sam Wyer

Printed and bound by Marston Book Services Limited, Didcot.

Converted by CPI Group (UK) Ltd, Croydon, CR0 4YY.

Introduction

BY WRITER/CO-DIRECTOR OLIVER LANSLEY

The idea for *The Trench* arrived in the van on the way home from the Edinburgh Festival 2011. My co-director James Seager and I began the journey, as all journeys home from the Edinburgh begin, with the vow that we wouldn't do the festival again the following year. (2012 will be Les Enfants Terribles' 11th in a row!)

By the end of the journey we had the idea for a new show.

We discussed the sort of thing we wanted to do. I wanted to write something magical, a quest; inspired by the great fantasies like *Alice in Wonderland* – a new world to explore. James mentioned the idea of the trenches of World War One and suddenly we had found our rabbit hole. What other place ever offered such a desperate need for escape?

Researching the subject of World War One tunnellers was fascinating and the discovery of the story of real-life tunneller William Hackett was a real inspiration. The only tunneller ever to receive the Victoria Cross, he was a fascinating character. When the war started he was desperate to do his bit, but at 41 he was considered too old for the Infantry and was refused three times.

Eventually when tunnel warfare was increased William, a skilled miner, was called up.

On the morning of 22 June 1916, Sapper William Hackett and four other miners of 254 Tunnelling Company were driving a tunnel towards the enemy lines below the cratered surface of the Givenchy-en-Gohelle sector of northern France. At 2.50am the explosion of a heavy German mine (the Red Dragon) buried the man. When the rescue party arrived William Hackett helped three men to safety but refused to leave the seriously injured twenty-two-year-old Thomas Collins. Apparently his words were 'I am a tunneller, I must look after the others first'. The rescue tunnel collapsed and the two men were lost forever.

Though *The Trench* is not directly about William Hackett, he certainly served as a huge inspiration and all these names and images were swirling round my mind as I wrote.

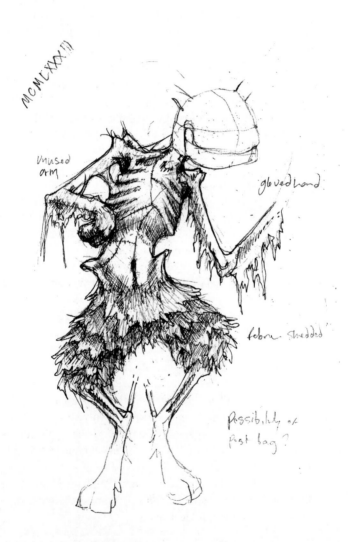

MCMLXXX?!

unused
arm

gloved hand.

fabric shredded

Possibility of
first bag?

The idea digested for a long time, and I attempted to write it several times but something just wouldn't click. I had initially envisaged it as a straightforward play, but whenever I wrote the dialogue it never seemed weighty enough for its subject matter. Also the mixture of the ultra-real world of the trench and the magical world created when Bert descends into the tunnels were very hard to reconcile with one another. It was half gritty realism and half fantasy, and the stakes were so huge; life, death, love, war, sacrifice. I needed to somehow distil these themes into a more personal journey.

The story of Orpheus in the underworld was stuck in my mind, the man who loved his wife so much he travelled to the Underworld to try and bring her back. This was the sort of story I wanted to write, essentially a Greek tragedy. I toyed with an idea of a Greek chorus, and when I started looking at World War One poetry it all seemed to fall into place.

Suddenly the form gave me the ability to be as epic as I felt the story was crying out for. I started writing, then just kept on going, the imagery and ideas just pouring onto the page. What began as a chorus prologue, continued to become a fifteen page verse poem.

It ended up being a far more personal piece than I had anticipated and despite it being set in one of the bleakest periods of our history, it became a story of salvation. This is possibly because it is only when we are tested the most, that the scale of potential within the human spirit can really come to light.

I must also take this opportunity to thank the sublimely talented Alexander Wolfe whose haunting and stunningly beautiful music is the most wonderful companion to the piece that I could ever wish for.

The Trench is dedicated to William Hackett and Thomas Collins, and every individual who lost their lives during The 'Great' War. May we never forget the horrors they witnessed and the sacrifices they made.

Acknowledgements:
Malcolm and Gillian Lansley, Vicky Sanders, Malcolm and Jean Sanders, Luton Hat Factory, Wales Millennium Centre, The Pleasance, South Nutfield Scout Hut, Sally Higginson, Tom Attwood, Elise Colledge, Harriet Darling, Megan Harrison, Lara Booth, Isabella Van Braeckel, Georgi Shire, Richard Mansfield, The Gate Theatre, Jude Christian, Natalie Richardson and Alex McCarthy.

Introduction

BY CO-DIRECTOR JAMES SEAGER

I have always been hugely fascinated with the First World War ever since I first visited the battlefields on a school trip. Nothing can quite compare you for the scale, brutality and sheer number of those who gave their lives; Tyne Cot cemetery in Belgium alone is a truly moving experience where over 12,000 commonwealth soldiers are buried. The war itself is also extremely interesting in that it really represented a shift in technology and warfare itself – this was the first war to use planes, tanks, modern guns and yet at the same time was paradoxically almost medieval in the idea of digging trenches and literally advancing on an enemies' position into machine gun fire when called upon to do so. It was also the war that enforced conscription and I always thought that if I had been born in that time I would have been fighting without a choice and statistically, probably not making it!

Because of this interest I've always wanted to set a play in the trenches; it's an incredibly evocative time period with countless stories of bravery and sacrifice. However, in talking to Oli, we as a company obviously wanted to do something a little different and something that fitted our style and ethos. I always liked the idea of someone being stuck somehow and in trying to find an escape, venturing off into a strange, bizarre world.

Oli started working on idea and for me there were three key moments in its development: firstly, his discovery of the true story of a miner who became entombed in the tunnels; secondly, the influencing of the classic Greek stories, like *Orpheus in the Underworld*, and finally the thought that the whole play could be an epic verse poem. Turning the story into a poem was a key moment as it allowed further links to the many world war poets that existed, and seemed to be the major source of expression for the horror that was witnessed.

Once the poem had been completed the next problem presented itself – turning it in to a play! I wanted to emphasise the isolation of the central character Bert when he becomes trapped, and so switching the narration on to Bert at the pivotal point in the story seemed to be a good way for the audience to really focus on Bert and his struggle. We always discussed the other characters being a mix of a Greek

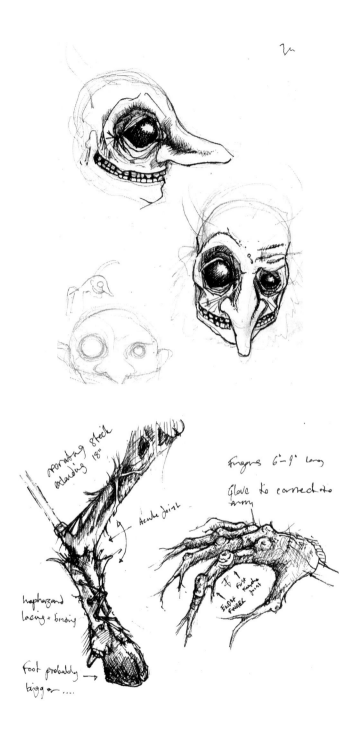

2.

operating steel
extending 18"

Acute Joint

haphazard
lacing + binding

foot probably
bigger ....

fingers 6"-9" long

Glove to connected to
army

Elbow
FINGER

first
Knuckle
Joint

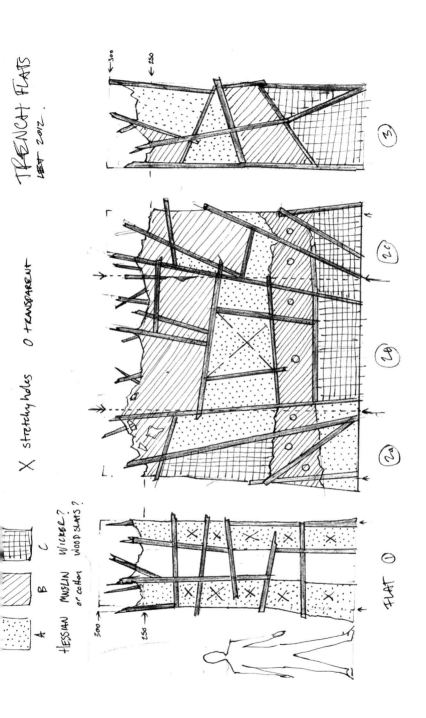

TRENCH FLATS
LEET 2012.

X stretchy holes   O TRANSPARENT

A HESSIAN   B MUSLIN or cotton   C WICKER? WOOD SLATS?

FLAT ①

←300
←250

②a   ②b   ②c

③
←300
←250

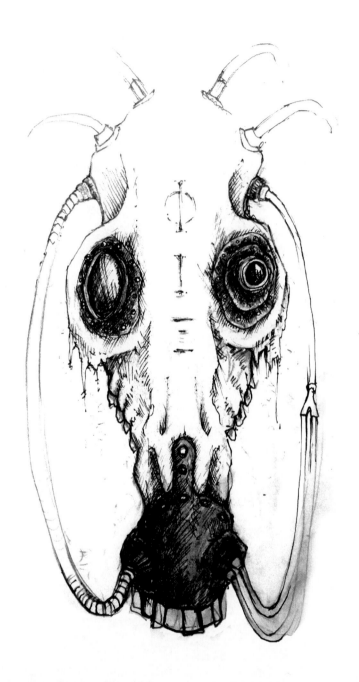

Les Enfants Terribles

'As the name of his company suggests, Oliver Lansley of Les
Enfants Terribles has actually found that winning formula of
talent, charm and absolute irreverence – think, really cool top of
the class kid.'
The Stage

'Razor sharp theatre group Les Enfants Terribles' (*The Telegraph*)
are dedicated to creating original, innovative and exciting theatre
that challenges, inspires and entertains. We are constantly pushing
ourselves to explore and develop new techniques and methods to tell
stories whilst at the heart of our work always remaining accessible to
our audience and ever growing fanbase. Born out of genuine passion
and excitement for creating theatre, we are always keen to find new
ways of immersing ourselves and our audiences into the weird and
wonderful worlds created by our shows.

Founded by Artistic Director Oliver Lansley in 2001, the company
has continued to grow and receive consistent critical acclaim, been
nominated for and won top industry awards, and established a large
and loyal following for its original and unique work. The company
has performed productions to thousands of people all over the world
including theatres in Australia, the Czech Republic, Dubai, Norway,
Poland, Singapore and has toured extensively all over the UK.

Long-time collaborator James Seager came on board as associate
producer to help run the company in 2005.

In its ten-year history the company has gone from performing
in 50-seat venues on a shoestring budget to working consistently in
large-scale venues, building a considerable critical and commercial
following and touring the globe with its fresh and innovative
productions.

Les Enfants Terribles have now built a reputation for being one of
the most visually exciting British theatre companies working today.

'A talented company with a very sure sense
of its own distinctive storytelling style.'
The Guardian

Oliver Lansley

Oliver is Founder and Artistic Director of Les Enfants Terribles Theatre Company. He also writes all of the company's output. Oliver has worked successfully in theatre, film and television, is a past winner of Channel Four's/4Talent's Multi-Talented Award and also a *Broadcast* magazine 'Hotshot'. A published playwright, his play *Immaculate* (2006) was listed in the top ten bestselling plays at Samuel French London in 2010. In 2011 his *Les Enfants Terribles: Collected Plays* was published by Oberon books, along with a number of other titles including *Flies* and *The Infant*. Oliver has seen his work produced all around the world as well as being translated into several different languages.

Previous plays for LET include *The Terrible Infants* and *Ernest and the Pale Moon*. His television writing work includes *Whites*, co-created and written with Matt King and described as 'a perfect example of the modern sitcom' (*The Times*). He also co-wrote and created the Rose D'or nominated ITV2 series *FM* – 'The greatest radio comedy since *Frasier*' (*The Metro*) and is currently working on several television projects. Oliver's film and television directing credits include *Alan Davies' Little Cracker* for Sky Television and the short *Stuck Under September*. He is currently developing further film projects. As an actor, Oliver has worked across film, television and theatre, most notably playing Kenny Everett in the BBC4 film of his life *The Best Possible Taste*. Other TV credits include, *Whites*, *FM*, *Holby City* and *EastEnders*. Theatre credits include playing Eddy in Berkoff's *Greek* at the Riverside Studios to lead roles in the numerous LET productions he has toured nationally and internationally with, including: *The Infant*, *The Terrible Infants*, *Ernest and the Pale Moon* and *The Vaudevillains*.

THE TRENCH

Characters

BERT

DEMON

COLLINS

GUIDE

SOLDIER 1

SOLDIER 2

CHORUS 1

CHORUS 2

CHORUS 3

The Trench first premiered at the Edinburgh Fringe in 2012 at Pleasance Two in The Pleasance Courtyard.

It was produced and created by Les Enfants Terribles Theatre Company in association with Wales Millennium Centre and Luton Hat Factory.

Cast list in order of appearance:

BERT: Oliver Lansley
CHORUS 1 / SOLDIER 1: Conrad Sharp
CHORUS 2 / COLLINS / GUIDE: Alfie Boyd
CHORUS 3 / DEMON / SOLDIER 2: Tim Jackson

All music written and played live by Alexander Wolfe

Director: Oliver Lansley & James Seager
Designer: Sam Wyer
Lighting Designer: Paul Green
Music by: Alexander Wolfe
Animation by: Richard Mansfield (www.muckypuppets.co.uk)

The Trench – Poem

In time long passed but not to be forgot
A battle raged across our fragile earth.
A generation's youth ripped cruel away.
Both sons and fathers buried side by side.
Forced to kill or be killed in return.
To blindly fight on King and country's whim.
A species on its own extinction's brink.
A waste too monstrous e'er to comprehend.
The future's youth may never understand
The hell that once descended 'pon this place.
They can but swear to honour fallen men
And pray such horrors never come again.

Deep underneath the unplanned graves of those
Whose precious lives were offered up like bait.
Far down below the thick and oily mud,
We find the men who trudge toward their fate.
They crawl upon their bellies, inch by inch.
They scrape the clay, and breathe the stale air.
They listen out for sounds from other men,
Who seek to find them out and trap them there.
Each moment living with the heavy fact
That where they lie may yet become their grave.
As earth and weight and tragic circumstance
Does heavy from above, upon them weigh.
Down here we find a man, Herbert his name.
Who half his life was spent beneath the earth.
A miner, born and bred, through father's past.
Now finds himself beneath a field in France.
To dig out holes beneath the en'my feet
and lay the charges sent down from on high.
Who deemed death from above was not enough
And seek out other ways to kill young men.

A simple man with simple tastes is he,
Who not once dreamt of shirking from this fate.
Three times he volunteered but was refused,
As Drs' claimed his heart had not the strength
To cope with all the stress that lay ahead.
But seeing men much younger than himself
All shipped to foreign fields and left to die.
He felt the burden of his country's call.
And could not rest until he played his part.
And so he persevered until the day
When stock of younger blood was running low,
And he was offered up his chance to die,
to help his country deal another blow.

So off he went with noble, brave intent
To serve his King and country with a smile.
But as each day of war was cruelly scratched
into his consciousness like many scars,
His sense of life began to ebb away
Fresh horrors witnessed, each and every day.
Eyes for eyes and teeth for teeth exchanged
And from that moment forth the world had changed.

His eyes will never close from what he's seen
Nor will his ears be free from sounds that crawl
Down deep inside his mind just like the lice
who burrow far beneath his rotting skin.
And refuse to be removed, through wash or fire
Or fumigation, always to return.

Never will he leave this place behind.
For though his battered body lives to fight,
The light of life within has been put out.
And now he lives in fear of simple sleep
For when the darkness comes he can but weep.

A life of digging tunnels took its toll.
The daily toil was back-breaking and bleak.
Our hero Herbert passed his time alone.
His trudging progress measured inch by inch.
His days began to melt like wax into
One endless stretch of hours undefined.
When sun and moon are taken from your sight
The days refuse to keep their fixed address.
And time becomes a landscape, featureless.
A distance to be crossed and nothing more.
The thought that kept a spark within his breast
Was simply that of wife at home in wait.

Her belly swelled with life grown from his seed.
A child, a hope that from this sea of death
New life may grow, who'll never see such sights.
And may, from predecessors legion faults,
Learn ways to live instead of ways to die.

Upon one indistinguishable day
A private Collins joined him in his hole.
A fresh faced boy of barely seventeen.
Who volunteered while flushed with boyish pride
To find himself alone in fields of France,
A rifle thrust into his soft-skinned hand.
With orders, loose, to shoot at other boys.
Or give his life to gain a foot of soil.

The two men, who in normal course of life,
Would find no common ground on which to walk.
Did quickly strike a fine resounding chord
And friendship crackled spritely into life.

Bert said the boy recalled him of himself,
Though in truth there was no likeness to be found.
As Bert had always carried with him weight.
A strength of mind beyond his earthly years.
While Collins was a newly crafted soul
A boy untainted by the truth of life.

The pair had been entrusted with the role
To dig under the no man's land above.
And lay the charges under en'my lines
To give their soldiers hope in hopeless times.

As Foe and Foe grew closer inch by inch
saturating land through which they passed.
A heavy sense of fate began to swell

As all must have an end that has a start.
There soon would come a point where two sides meet.
A moment where each smash against the wall.
And in that moment time will come undone,
And faces who've been grown to love will fall.

Bert and Collins worked beneath the mud,
in warrens unfit for the use of men.
Deceived by false protectiveness of dark,
And distance from the angry world above.
They passed the hours with talk of life forgot,
Of trifles, mere and minuscule in scale.
Such conversation served to keep them sane,
With dreams of life that bore no consequence.

They know not that a dragon sleeps nearby,
Whose fiery breath will consume all it finds.
An en'my mine, lays dormant in the mud
Placed there by men no different from themselves.
It waits there for the time to bare its teeth
And open jaws to swallow from beneath.

The fateful day, which felt like those before
Whilst Herbert listened patient to the earth.
He heard a noise that quickly caught his breath
And chilled the very blood inside his veins.
Through mud and slime the noise began to reach
Of en'my footsteps moving in retreat.
He knew this movement sadly all too well
As chaos always followed swift behind.

Collecting thoughts he knew he must escape
and turned toward the tunnels open mouth.
But through the dark he saw with swift approach
The body of young Collins rushing forth.

His eyes were wide, his mouth stretched to a grin
And in his youthful grip an envelope.
'It's news from home' he cried with bubbling glee.
'The baby must have come! Quick look and see'.

Without a thought Bert grabbed the envelope
And swiftly tore the letter from within.
But as his eyes scanned through the written words
He felt a pain begin to grip his heart.

His breath was choked as from the page he read
The news laid out in unfamiliar hand.

His dearest wife in act of giving birth
Had suffered complications most severe.
The loss of blood preceded loss of life
And loss of both things that he held most dear.
A future, in an instant disappeared.

But before these words could settle in Bert's mind
A shattering blow, smashed heavy through the air.
The Dragon had been woken from its sleep
And loosed a roar that shook their very souls.

A sound like nothing ever heard before
echoed off the tunnel's fragile walls.
Then swiftly followed heavy weight of dirt
That sought to bury bodies where they stood.
Thick chunks of clay struck hard like cannonballs
Crushing limbs and cracking bones at will.
Drowning deep beneath the detritus
Entombed forever underneath the mud.

Fin'lly the silence came, as earth exhaled
And darkness settled calmly over all.

From deep within his coffin made of dirt
The body of Bert lay as if asleep.
His consciousness ebbed in and out like waves
Perhaps unsure if ever he should wake
or gently let the airless dark consume
and let the horrors end forever more.

But something in his soul refused to sleep.
An ember glowing, not to be put out.

A piercing scream rings loud amidst the dark
And Bert awakes to find himself alone...

At first survival instinct acts alone.
And checks are made to see what's still intact.
Each leg and arm and finger move in turn.
Then skin is traced for open rips and tears
And source of any hot blood tightly bound.

The blackness that surrounds is thick and full
And not a crack of light finds its way in.
Though creeps a gentle breeze from some air pipe
Somehow left intact despite the blast.

'Collins?' Fall the words from out his lips,
his ringing ears strain fiercely for reply.
'Collins, are you there?' he shouts aloud
His once strong voice now cracking to a cry.

The empty sound that shouts back in his face
Sounds hollow as it drifts across his skin.
The silence drowning out the piercing tone
left shrieking in his weak and ruptured drums.

His fingers fumble 'cross the filthy ground
In search of something that could be of use.
Instead they land upon an envelope
and recollections of the last words read...

As piece by piece a clarity returns
And with it desperate thoughts like bullets hit.
He wishes from his soul that he had died
And not survived to let such hellish news
Be recalled in his mind a second time.
A fresh bereavement hits his heart once more.
And now he thinks this darkness must be hell.
Encased in blackness, haunted by his loss.

A sound from out his guts rings through the air
A cry of wounded creature, bleak and torn.
And boiling tears weep heavy from his eyes
While sobs shake hard like blows upon his ribs.

In that one moment everything is gone
and to the covered heavens he does cry
for answers to this Godless misery.
The word that sticks upon his lips is *Why?'*

And there and then he offers up his soul
As payment in return for others lost.
A plea for remedy to poison drunk.
A promise to agree to any cost.

And lo, these fevered prayers don't go unheard
For through the darkness comes a rasping voice.
A click of hooves through mud approaches slow
The shadow of a figure stoops in sight.

And peeling open sore and salty eyes,
A frantic Bert takes grip upon himself.
He stares into the murky dark ahead
Afire with fear and hope in equal parts.
 'I can help you find the thing you seek'
The creature speaks with steady tone and eye.
'But as with every other thing in life
be known with all that's taken comes a price.'

Bert eyes the creature, humped and cloven hoofed
Its black eyes shine like puddles in the mud.

And all his fear falls from his weary bones
And crawling to his feet he calmly says.
'There is no cost more great than that I've paid'.

The creature nods and flickers with a smile,
'Then offer help I shall but first this know
the path ahead will not be straight to walk.
Three trials must you face along the way
To prove that you possess the heart and worth.'

The words clacked heavy from the creature's throat
Like bark shards flaking from an ancient tree.
Its skin like hides of gargoyles long forgot
All stitched and stretched to hide its crooked bones.

'The first to pass across an open field
that lies atop a sharp and thorny ridge.
Your pace must never pass beyond a walk
No matter what the fear within your heart.
And final word to keep you on your path
Whatever happens only look ahead.'

With that the thing withdraws into the dark,
Burt calls out but there comes back no reply.
He scrambles on the floor to find his lamp
But when he turns it on the beast has gone.

He looks around inside his darkened tomb
The heavy mud bears down like sagging skin.
But in the corner he spies something strange
Which makes the cogs inside his mind spin fast.

Bert had lived inside these halls for months
He knew each inch of soil like his home.
Yet there before his raw and salt-drenched eyes
An opening presented forth itself.
A tunnel mouth through which he'd never been
As if a sleeping serpent had awoke
And open'd jaws unto a world below.

He lifts his light and urges weary legs
To follow down the path that lay ahead.
The path is steep and leads him deeper still
Into the belly of the earth below.
And on he walks for what it seems like days
Until he reaches finally a stop.
And there before his eyes there lies a ridge
All covered over thick with vicious thorns.

Bert steels himself and with emboldened heart
He starts to climb the sheer and wiry slope.
Yet every time he grips the jagged vines
Their teeth do cut and sear his hardened palms.
The barbs gripped hard to all that they could find
Imploring Bert to go no further on.
But he ignores their rabid clutching teeth.
And even as the blood seeps 'cross his skin.
and body cries out from a thousand cuts
He ventures on until he finds the top.

Upon the summit comes an ounce of peace
As out he gazes 'cross the open field.
Ahead he sees the spot that he must reach
Barely a hundred yards were there to cross.

So off he sets at measured walking pace
He takes his first assured but cautious step.
When boot touched ground the feeling met was
strange
Its texture soft and giving more than most
But brittle-er than mud or sand it seemed.
Like hardened shells of eggs encased in cloth.

Yet several further forward steps he takes
And with the words that ring inside his ears
His eyes, as told, stay firmly fixed ahead.
Not once sneaking adrift to peer below.

But as he finds the centre of the field
An awful sound does start to prick his ears.
Like groans collective, seeping from the souls
Of lost folk, now awakened from cold sleep.
And with each step his boots do heavy grow
As ground below begins to snap and burst.

A sinking feeling rising in his chest
The old familiar stench crawls down his throat.

One final step he takes before he feels
A desperate grip that curls around his leg
The feel of human fingers clutching hold
The helpless plea of men been left for dead.

And nothing then could stop the instinct fierce
As eyes drop down to look below his feet.

And suddenly he finds himself transported
To back inside a memory so raw.
He feels the air of France fill up his lungs
And brightness of the sky stings sharp his eyes.

He stands upon a field where once grew grass,
Now only bloodied limbs do pierce the mud.
And bony fingers clutching fruitless stand,
Like stalks whose flowers long have disappeared.

Bert fights to hold the bile in his guts
And grips his legs to try and keep his feet.
A place he thought he'd left behind for good
A scene of hell sits fresh to be relived.

He closes eyes and bites down on his lip.
Remembering the words the creature spat.

*'Your pace must never pass beyond a walk
No matter what the fear within your heart.'*
He wanders slowly, heavy boots all caked,
And sodden as they break the earth below.
Like virgin snow, it crunches under foot,
As youth and dreams and loves are crushed beneath.

He walks on, at a measured pace, his fear
Paralysed underneath the weight of lead
That fills the air, and noise that fills his head.
On and on he walks, no end in sight.
The sounds of air expelled from lungs surrounds,
The smell of flesh, that bursts and burns confounds.
The flecks of blood and brain and bone that land
Upon his skin like snowflakes, hot with life
That once was full of possibility
but now just serves to fertilise the land.
Too many ghosts to haunt this empty place.

Bert breathes down to his boots and eyes ahead
He ushers forth each straw of strength he has
And step by step he finds the field's edge.

The moment that his feet do leave the mud.
The screeching sound of horror disappears.
And when he turns around to look behind
Nothing but an empty field he sees.

'*The first trial is complete*' rings out a voice.
And Bert turns round to see the beast's black eyes.
'*The second lies in wait should you proceed.*
But know that further horrors lurk ahead.'

Bert looks down at his hand to see it shake
As hot adrenalin pipes through his veins.
He catches breath and clenches weary fists.
Then forward steps, a steel within his heart.

'*Along this path a chamber you shall find.*
Wherein resides a strange and vivid beast.
Its riddle you must solve for you to pass.
But be sure to answer quick and answer true

For know within its breath a poison lies
Enough to send men mad and even worse.'

And with those words the creature holds his gaze
Then turns and shuffles into dark once more.

Bert grits his yellow teeth and presses on.
The dim and pitted path shows him the way.

Before too long the tunnels walls constrict
And Bert is forced to crawl that he may pass.
He feels the solid clay beneath his hands,
The crumbling earth that scrapes atop his head.
The roots of trees long dead reach down to stroke
his back as if to see if he is real.
He drudges through these bow-els of the world
'till up ahead he spies a yellow glow.
And out he's poured into a hollowed room
Where there ahead his greeter lies in wait.

The Demon's shape is hard to tell at first,
It seems to almost rise up from a mist.
A cloudy mustard hue its form doth take
And at the top a hard and fearsome face
That shakes Bert's nerve in cold and desp'rate fear.

Two empty eyes stare deep into his soul
like darkened portholes of a sunken ship.
And long and slender beak that stretches out
Like muz-zle of a horse but hard and sharp.
And through this trunk the wheezing sound of breath
Doth scrape like gravel poured upon a grate.

'You wish to pass?' the spectre hisses soft
and as he does Bert sees its breath expel
a dense mist that sits heavier than air.
Which creeps toward him sure and silently.
Bert looks down to his boots and notices,
The ground is slicked with oily residue.

He feels his skin begin to prick and burn
A sickness in his stomach starts to rise.
His eyes begin to itch and sting and swell
His throat feels raw, like stripped of all its flesh.

'If riddle you can solve you may proceed
But should you fail your grave be where you fall.'
And then the monster rose to its full height
And heaved its question from its poisoned lungs.

'What thing can sate a Warlord's appetite?
Or soothe a battle widow's broken heart?
What can bring back the sons and daughters lost?
Or makes the shed of blood seem justified?'

Bert feels the breath surround him like a fog,
His skin alight like fire, blister'd and cracked.
Metallic taste of blood crawls in his mouth
And ground feels like 'tis ripped from underneath.

He fixes on the words that sting his mind.
He pictures leaders mongering their wars.
The weeping wives when telegrams received
And parents losing that they held most dear.
He searches through all reason he might find
For end to justify these hateful means?

And in that moment he recalls his wife
And unborn baby cruelly ripped away.

He looks into the creature's deadened eyes
His hanging face, like a devil's sick of sin;
And suddenly the answer rings out clear.
And with his final ounce of breath he rasps:

'No thing can sate a Warlord's appetite
Or soothe a battle widow's broken heart.
No thing brings back the sons and daughters lost.
Or makes the shed of blood seem justified.

Nothing. That's the answer that you seek.'

And as those words escape Bert's crackened lips
The beast evaporates into the air.
Its heavy skull drops empty at Bert's feet.
Leaving just a cloak of mist behind.

With no breath left, Bert falls down to his knees
And pulls the creature's mask upon his face.
Then just like icy water from a spring
He swallows gulps of air and fills his lungs.
And through the windows of the creature's eyes
He finds his feet and passes through the fog.

He staggers further through the darkened lanes
His heart emboldened with each taken step.
His eyes adjusting to the lack of light
As if becoming part of this dark world.

The passage widens to a chambered hall
With pillars grand, stretched down from ancient roots
That twist and gnarl, like oaken limbs entwined
The bodies of the Gods laid down to sleep.

Set deep within the roots there lies a door.
That looks though it had stood since dawn of time.
And built either to keep unwanteds out
Or p'raps to hold something far worse inside.

Sitting high twixt the tangled webs of branch
The cloven creature watches blankly on.
'You've reached the final trial of your quest
and with it comes the chance to prove your worth.
Beyond this door a Guardian awaits
Who holds within the key to set you free.
This demon you must conquer to proceed
or else be trapped in dark forever more.'

And as he speaks the cumbrous door unlocks
And with the hoary creak of ancient wood,
it open creeps upon it's hefty hinge
revealing forth the path for Bert to take.

Bert summons all the stocks retained within
And presses forth once more upon his quest.
With leaden foot he trudges through the gloom
To hear the heavy door slam hard behind
And trap him with whatever lays within.

A few more careful steps he takes inside
And as his eyes adjust to the dim light
He recognises that in which he stands
And deep remembered fears grab swift ahold.

He finds himself stood in familiar trench
like that in which he'd lived for countless days.

The filthy, rutted duck-boards under foot
and sodden sandbags stacked against the mud.
The signs of soldiers littering the way.
A stench of death and excrement abides.
The pools of sludge all mixed with rum and blood,
Old boots, and rats and relics of those lost.
Endless wire, like barbed and bloody bunting
To celebrate the horrors all around.

Stood lurking in the dark of this foxhole.
Face obscured beneath its heavy helmet.
A figure hunches, fearsome in its sight.
Drenched in steely grey of En'my garb.

It turns to Bert, then without any thought
It lunges t'ward him, rabid in its pace.
Bert's instincts pull his hand towards his hip
But weapon was long lost along the way.

Before he even has the chance to think
The figure smashes heavily upon
And thrusts Bert's body hard into the mud
With fever only capable from man
Who knows kill or be killed is all that stands.

The du-el that doth follow hath no grace
There's no heroic ballet to behold.
Just feral, desp'rate, creatures battle-ing
Not for honour or country, just their life.

The stamp of boot, the hammer of a fist
thump dull against the living bone and flesh.
Fingers tear and gouge and rip and claw
And tighten roughly round opponents' necks.

Faces are pushed beneath the sickly mud
And sticks and bricks and elbows utilized
'Til fin'lly one man's will outlives his foe
And yet another light is doused with woe.

Bert's heart beats fast, his breath returns in waves
The blood that's on his hands is not his own.
No pride is there to take, nor victory
Just grudging continuity of breath.

He looks to where his fierce opponent lies
The evil brute his King taught him to hate
And reaching down pulls helmet from his head
To see the fearsome face that lies beneath.

But in the visage staring back at him
the features that he sees are of his own.
The youth that he once was lays at his feet
the fickle flame of life now fading fast.

Bert barely recognises in his eyes
The child that once existed in its place.
And all that he can do is hold him close
And comfort him as death's cold rattle shakes.
Tears come not, just emptiness resounds

Another penny falling in the drum.
There are no sobs within with which to grieve
No curses left to shriek into the sky.

But as Bert holds the broken body close
He feels its flesh surrounding start to shake.
The uniform begins to stretch and tear
as bones beneath begin to change their shape.
Bert takes a step away, his eyes awide
In disbelief at what he sees before.

Where once was skin now scales start to form
hard bony ridges piercing through its hide.
Where fingernails should be now claws emerge
And grows a tail, like serpent from the sea.
The face, no longer recognised as man
Shows snout and teeth and snarling, smoking breath
And fin'lly bursting from the creatures back
Two giant wings stretch forth like Angel's limbs.

The dragon turns to fix Bert with a stare
and like volcano spits forth floods of fire.
Then with a roar that shakes the ground below
It flaps its giant wings with all its might
And smashes through the earth over their heads
To burst forth to the heavens far above.

Bert stands below the newly opened hole
And feels a light shine down upon his face.

Then suddenly feels grip upon his arm
And sound of creatures from another time.
'Is that you Bert?' cries down familiar voice
'We're here to get you out, just take my hand,
we have to hurry cos this hole won't last
But just one final push and you'll be free.'

A hope stirs in Bert's soul he'd thought was lost
And suddenly the urge to live burns bright.
But as he tries to start his sweet ascent
A noise rings faintly from the dark below.
He turns his head and strains his ears to hear
And sure enough there comes a baby's cry.

Then letting go of saviour's hand above
Bert turns and disappears back to the gloom.

'*Bert!*' comes the cry that issues from above
'*The tunnel will not hold, we have to go!*'

But Bert ignores the warnings in his ears
and runs towards the infant's weeping wail,
until he finds a collapsed wooden beam
and body trapped and bleeding underneath.
'*My son*' he cries as tears prick at his eyes
and then with every ounce of strength he owns
he grips the wood and lifts with all his worth
And there below lies Collins still alive.

He grabs the boy and drags him through the mud
Whilst praying that he will not be too late.
'Til up ahead he spies the divine light
and hears the voices calling through the breach.

'*The tunnel's closing there's no time to spare
the earth's collapsing even as we speak.*'
Then Bert takes Collins tightly in his arms
And lifts his dear friend high above his head.
to pass him up into the waiting hands
and see him disappear into the light.

The men pull Collins up into their arms.
as tunnel falls and crumbles all around.
And as the boy emerges from the hole
The earth gives birth to yet another son.

Yet as is wont, with life must follow death
And Bert is swallowed by the dark anew.

He stands below in blackness once again
And feels the stale air round him start to thin.
He shuts his eyes and leans against the mud,
His body weak, his breath begins to slow.
And as he, weary, submits to the end.
A gentle smile flickers 'cross his face.

'You passed the final test' calls out a voice
And from the dark steps his unearthly guide
'You've shown the strength of heart which you possess
and proved you're worthy of that which you seek
You willing, gave the price that you were asked.
Now time has come for you to claim your prize.'

The creature nods then turns upon its heel
And with one final look he disappears.

Then from the black a glow begins to swell
and figure dressed in white starts to emerge.
Bert rubs his salty eyes and takes a breath
As with each step the angel grows more clear.
'Til soon before him stands his darling wife.
And in her arms a beaut'ful babe doth sleep.

She puts her hand upon Bert's trembling cheek
And whispers tender words into his ear.
Bert looks down to the infant in her arms
And feels his heart swell deep within his chest.
Then with one perfect kiss she takes his hand
And leads him gently t'ward the brilliant light.

And with each step Bert takes, a weight doth lift
As ling'ring fear begins to loose its grip.
The smell of death starts fading from his lungs
The sight of blood clean washes from his eyes
The cry of bombs and guns begin to cease
And fin'lly Bert lets go, at last at peace.

The End.

Prologue

The actor playing BERT delivers the opening prologue.

> In time long passed but not to be forgot
> A battle raged across our fragile earth.
> A generation's youth ripped cruel away.
> Both sons and fathers buried side by side.
> Forced to kill or be killed in return.
> To blindly fight on King and country's whim.
> A species on its own extinction's brink.
> A waste too monstrous e'er to comprehend.
> The future's youth may never understand
> The hell that once descended 'pon this place.
> They can but swear to honour fallen men
> And pray such horrors never come again.

We hear the sound of a flare go up and the stage is bathed in red light and smoke; revealing for the first time that we are in the cross section of a stylised Trench. We hear the distant sound and flashes of guns and explosions.

'THE LANDING' STRING INTRODUCTION starts to play.

We reveal the CHORUS all sitting, huddled at the bottom of the Trench amongst the sandbags. They slowly emerge into the light.

CHORUS 1	Deep underneath the unplanned graves of those Whose precious lives were offered up like bait.
CHORUS 2	Far down below the thick and oily mud,
CHORUS 3	We find the men who trudge toward their fate.
CHORUS 1	They crawl upon their bellies, inch by inch.
CHORUS 3	They scrape the clay,
CHORUS 2	and breathe the stale air.
CHORUS 1	They listen out for sounds from other men,

CHORUS 3	Who seek to find them out and trap them there.
CHORUS 2	Each moment living with the heavy fact That where they lie may yet become their grave.
CHORUS 3	As earth...
CHORUS 1	...and weight
CHORUS 2	and tragic circumstance
CHORUS 1	Does heavy from above, upon them weigh.

First Verse – 'THE LANDING'

From inside the structure, behind gauze, BERT is lit and we see him, crawling slowly through a tiny claustrophobic space.

ANIMATION 1. *The cross section of the tunnel is animated, the occasional drop of dirt falls down.*

CHORUS 2	Down here we find a man,
CHORUS 3	Herbert his name.
CHORUS 1	Who half his life was spent beneath the earth.
CHORUS 2	A miner, born and bred, through father's past.
CHORUS 1	Now finds himself beneath a field in France.
CHORUS 3	To dig out holes beneath the en'my feet
CHORUS 1	and lay the charges sent down from on high. Who deemed death from above was not enough
CHORUS 2	And seek out other ways to kill young men.

CHORUS – 'LANDING'

BERT breaks through the gauze. The CHORUS hold up a plank which he crawls on to, they bring him out and manipulate him like a puppet in front of the audience.

The CHORUS use the planks throughout the next section.

| CHORUS 1 | A simple man with simple tastes is he,
Who not once dreamt of shirking from this fate. |

CHORUS 3	Three times he volunteered but was refused,
CHORUS 1	As Dr's claimed his heart had not the strength To cope with all the stress that lay ahead.
CHORUS 3	But seeing men much younger than himself All shipped to foreign fields and left to die.
CHORUS 2	He felt the burden of his country's call.
CHORUS 1	And could not rest until he played his part.
CHORUS 2	And so he persevered until the day
CHORUS 1	When stock of younger blood was running low,
CHORUS 3	And he was offered up his chance to die, to help his country deal another blow.

The CHORUS and BERT gather their lanterns and move forwards.

CHORUS 2	So off he went with noble, brave intent To serve his King and country with a smile.
CHORUS 1	But as each day of war was cruelly scratched into his consciousness like many scars,

He extinguishes his light.

CHORUS 3	His sense of life began to ebb away Fresh horrors witnessed, each and every day.

He extinguishes his light.

CHORUS 2	Eyes for eyes and teeth for teeth exchanged And from that moment forth the world had changed.

He extinguishes his light.

Only BERT's lantern remains lit.

CHORUS 3	His eyes will never close from what he's seen
CHORUS 1	Nor will his ears be free from sounds that crawl Down deep inside his mind

CHORUS 2	just like the lice
	who burrow far beneath his rotting skin.
CHORUS 3	And refuse to be removed, through wash

The CHORUS slowly approaches BERT.

CHORUS 1	or fire
CHORUS 2	Or fumigation,
CHORUS 3	always to return.
CHORUS 2	Never will he leave this place behind.
CHORUS 1	For though his battered body lives to fight,
	The light of life within has been put out.
CHORUS 3	And now he lives in fear of simple sleep
	For when the darkness comes he can but weep.

BERT's light is finally extinguished. Darkness.

In the black we hear BERT's pickaxe, striking against the rock.

A percussive soundscape starts to build under the following as slowly the lights fade up.

| CHORUS 2 | A life of digging tunnels took its toll. |
| | The daily toil was back-breaking and bleak. |

CHORUS MEMBER 2 joins in the beat by brushing his boots.

CHORUS 1	Our hero Herbert passed his time alone.
	His trudging progress measured inch by inch.
	His days began to melt like wax into
	One endless stretch of hours undefined.

CHORUS MEMBER 1 joins the beat by loading and cocking his gun.

CHORUS 3	When sun and moon are taken from your sight
	The days refuse to keep their fixed address.
	And time becomes a landscape, featureless.
	A distance to be crossed and nothing more.

CHORUS MEMBER 3 finally joins in with an accordion.

The soundscape builds into the following song – 'WEIGHT OF THE WORLD'

ANIMATION 2. *A shadow of BERT with his pickaxe which slowly pulls out to reveal the tunnel. It pulls further out to see soldiers marching above. Then further and further until we reveal the world with two armies trudging inevitably towards each other.*

We then zoom right back down to BERT and into his head, where we dissolve into…

Heartbeat – 'WIFE THEME' – ('ONE BY ONE' introduction)

ANIMATION 3. *Wife silhouette; we see a baby in her stomach, heartbeat.*

CHORUS 2   The thought that kept a spark within his breast
             Was simply that of wife at home in wait.
             Her belly swelled with life grown from his seed.
             A child, a hope that from this sea of death
             New life may grow, who'll never see such sights.
             And may, from predecessors legion faults,
             Learn ways to live instead of ways to die.

Introduce COLLINS. The remaining CHORUS manipulates the planks and ammunition tins to create a cross section of a tunnel.

CHORUS 3   Upon one indistinguishable day
             A private Collins joined him in his hole.

CHORUS 1   A fresh faced boy of barely seventeen.
             Who volunteered while flushed with boyish pride
             To find himself alone in fields of France,

CHORUS 3   A rifle thrust into his soft skinned hand.
             With orders, loose, to shoot at other boys.

CHORUS 1   Or give his life to gain a foot of soil.

COLLINS clumsily sits next to BERT, continually and accidentally pointing his rifle at him.

CHORUS 3   The two men, who in normal course of life,
             Would find no common ground on which to walk.

> Did quickly strike a fine resounding chord
> And friendship crackled spritely into life.

CHORUS 1   Bert said the boy recalled him of himself,
Though in truth there was no likeness to be found.
As Bert had always carried with him weight.
A strength of mind beyond his earthly years.

CHORUS 3   While Collins was a newly crafted soul
A boy untainted by the truth of life.

The CHORUS lay the planks over them to form a tunnel.

CHORUS 1   The pair had been entrusted with the role
To dig under the no man's land above.

CHORUS 3   And lay the charges under en'my lines
To give their soldiers hope in hopeless times.

The CHORUS produce toy soldiers on top of the plank above BERT and COLLINS, then proceed to move them around like generals in a war room.

CHORUS 1   As Foe and Foe grew closer inch by inch
saturating land through which they passed.

CHORUS 3   A heavy sense of fate began to swell
As all must have an end that has a start.

CHORUS 1   There soon would come a point where two sides
meet.

CHORUS 3   A moment where each smash against the wall.

CHORUS 1   And in that moment time will come undone,

CHORUS 3   And faces who've been grown to love will fall.

The top plank is removed and the toy soldiers fall on BERT and COLLINS.

CHORUS 1   Bert and Collins lived beneath the mud,
in warrens unfit for the use of men.

CHORUS 3   Deceived by false protectiveness of dark,
And distance from the angry world above.

CHORUS 1	They passed the hours with talk of life forgot,
	Of trifles, mere and minuscule in scale.
CHORUS 3	Such conversation served to keep them sane,
	With dreams of life that bore no consequence.
CHORUS 1	They know not that a dragon sleeps nearby,
	Whose fiery breath will consume all it finds.
	An en'my mine, lays dormant in the mud
	Placed there by men no different from themselves.
CHORUS 3	It waits there for the time to bare its teeth
	And open jaws to swallow from beneath.

The planks are moved in to an arch above BERT.

CHORUS 1	The fateful day, which felt like those before
CHORUS 3	Whilst Herbert listened patient to the earth.
CHORUS 1	He heard a noise that quickly caught his breath
CHORUS 3	And chilled the very blood inside his veins.
CHORUS 1	Through mud
CHORUS 3	and slime
CHORUS 1	the noise began to reach
	Of en'my footsteps moving in retreat.
CHORUS 3	He knew this movement sadly all too well
CHORUS 1	As chaos always followed swift behind.
CHORUS 3	Collecting thoughts he knew he must escape
	and turned toward the tunnels open mouth.

As BERT turns, the planks spin to form the sides of the tunnel.

CHORUS 1	But through the dark he saw with swift approach
	The body of young Collins rushing forth.

COLLINS appears at the top of the Trench.

CHORUS 3	His eyes were wide,
CHORUS 1	his mouth stretched to a grin

CHORUS 3	And in his youthful grip…
CHORUS 1	…an envelope.
COLLINS	'It's news from home'
CHORUS 3	He cried with bubbling glee.
COLLINS	'The baby must have come! Quick look and see'.
CHORUS 1	Without a thought Bert grabbed the envelope And swiftly tore the letter from within.

The CHORUS surrounds BERT, reading the letter with him.

CHORUS 3	But as his eyes scanned through the written words
CHORUS 1	He felt a pain begin to grip his heart.
CHORUS 3	His breath was choked as from the page he read The news laid out in unfamiliar hand.
CHORUS 1	His dearest wife in act of giving birth Had suffered complications most severe. The loss of blood preceded loss of life And loss of both things that he held most dear. A future, in an instant disappeared.
CHORUS 3	But before these words could settle in Bert's mind A shattering blow, smashed heavy through the air.

'WEIGHT OF THE WORLD' – EXPLOSION BEGINS

Suddenly the Trench starts to collapse, the centre panel falls and the two side flats are lifted and slowly spun to create the effect of the explosion.

CHORUS 1	The Dragon had been woken from its sleep And loosed a roar that shook their very souls.
CHORUS 2	A sound like nothing ever heard before echoed off the tunnel's fragile walls.
CHORUS 3	Then swiftly followed heavy weight of dirt That sought to bury bodies where they stood.

CHORUS 1   Thick chunks of clay struck hard like cannonballs

CHORUS 2   Crushing limbs

CHORUS 3   and cracking bones at will.

CHORUS 1   Drowning deep beneath the detritus

CHORUS 3   Entombed forever underneath the mud.

'WEIGHT OF THE WORLD' – EXPLOSION BUILDS TO IT'S CLIMAX

The flats finally land on top of BERT, so only his hand is visible – creating the scene of the collapsed tunnel.

'IN BROAD DAYLIGHT'

A puppet of BERT's WIFE is manipulated beautifully in a dance over the song.

When the song finishes BERT's hand moves. He's alive. He struggles out from underneath the flats. BERT then takes over the narration.

BERT   At first survival instinct acts alone.
                  And checks are made to see what's still intact.
                  Each leg and arm and finger move in turn.
                  Then skin is traced for open rips and tears
                  And source of any hot blood tightly bound.

                  The blackness that surrounds is thick and full
                  And not a crack of light finds its way in.
                  Though creeps a gentle breeze from some air pipe
                  Somehow left intact despite the blast.

                  '*Collins?*' fall the words from out his lips,
                  his ringing ears strain fiercely for reply.
                  '*Collins, are you there?*' he shouts aloud
                  His once strong voice now cracking to a cry.

                  The empty sound that shouts back in his face
                  Sounds hollow as it drifts across his skin.
                  The silence drowning out the piercing tone
                  left shrieking in his weak and ruptured drums.

His fingers fumble 'cross the filthy ground
In search of something that could be of use.
Instead they land upon an envelope
and recollections of the last words read…

As piece by piece a clarity returns
And with it desperate thoughts like bullets hit.
He wishes from his soul that he had died
And not survived to let such hellish news

Be recalled in his mind a second time.
A fresh bereavement hits his heart once more.
And now he thinks this darkness must be hell.
Encased in blackness, haunted by his loss.

A sound from out his guts rings through the air
A cry of wounded creature, bleak and torn.
And boiling tears weep heavy from his eyes
While sobs shake hard like blows upon his ribs.

In that one moment everything is gone
and to the covered heavens he does cry
for answers to this Godless misery.
The word that sticks upon his lips is *'Why?'*

And there and then he offers up his soul
As payment in return for others lost.
A plea for remedy to poison drunk.
A promise to agree to any cost.

And lo, these fevered prayers don't go unheard
For through the darkness comes a rasping voice.
A click of hooves through mud approaches slow
The shadow of a figure stoops in sight.

'MAYFLOWERS' – GUIDE THEME

THE GUIDE puppet appears.

And peeling open sore and salty eyes,
A frantic Bert takes grip upon himself.
He stares into the murky dark ahead
Afire with fear and hope in equal parts.

GUIDE   *'I can help you find the thing you seek'*

CHORUS 3   The creature speaks with steady tone and eye.

GUIDE   *'But as with every other thing in life*
                be known with all that's taken comes a price.'

BERT   Bert eyes the creature, humped and cloven hoofed
                Its black eyes shine like puddles in the mud.
                And all his fear falls from his weary bones
                And crawling to his feet he calmly says.

                'There is no cost more great than that I've paid'.

CHORUS 1   The creature nods and flickers with a smile,

GUIDE   *'Then offer help I shall but first this know*
                the path ahead will not be straight to walk.
                Three trials must you face along the way
                To prove that you possess the heart and worth.'

CHORUS 3   The words clacked heavy from the creature's throat
                Like bark shards flaking from an ancient tree.

CHORUS 1   Its skin like hides of gargoyles long forgot
                All stitched and stretched to hide its crooked bones.

GUIDE   *'The first to pass across an open field*
                that lies atop a sharp and thorny ridge.
                Your pace must never pass beyond a walk
                No matter what the fear within your heart.
                And final word to keep you on your path
                Whatever happens only look ahead.'

CHORUS 3   With that the thing withdraws into the dark,

BERT   Bert calls out but there comes back no reply.
                He scrambles on the floor to find his lamp
                But when he turns it on the beast has gone.

He looks around inside his darkened tomb
The heavy mud bears down like sagging skin.
But in the corner he spies something strange
Which makes the cogs inside his mind spin fast.

Bert had lived inside these halls for months
He knew each inch of soil like his home.
Yet there before his raw and salt-drenched eyes

'DINOSAUR SONG' BEGINS

The flats are lifted to create a tunnel mouth.

An opening presented forth itself.
A tunnel mouth through which he'd never been
As if a sleeping serpent had awoke
And open'd jaws unto a world below.

He lifts his light and urges weary legs
To follow down the path that lay ahead.

ANIMATION 4. *BERT travelling deeper and deeper underground.*

Over the song BERT walks through the tunnels in controlled slow motion.

The path is steep and leads him deeper still
Into the belly of the earth below.

'DINOSAUR SONG' - CHORUS

And on he walks for what it seems like days
Until he reaches finally a stop.
And there before his eyes there lies a ridge
All covered over thick with vicious thorns.

Bert steels himself and with emboldened heart
He starts to climb the sheer and wiry slope.

The CHORUS form the thorny ridge and BERT clambers over them.

Yet every time he grips the jagged vines
Their teeth do cut and sear his hardened palms.
The barbs gripped hard to all that they could find

Imploring Bert to go no further on.
But he ignores their rabid clutching teeth.
And even as the blood seeps 'cross his skin.
and body cries out from a thousand cuts
He ventures on until he finds the top.

Upon the summit comes an ounce of peace
As out he gazes 'cross the open field.
Ahead he sees the spot that he must reach
Barely a hundred yards were there to cross.

So off he sets at measured walking pace
He takes his first assured but cautious step.

As BERT takes a step, the CHORUS move him backwards to the structure.

When boot touched ground the feeling met was
strange
Its texture soft and giving more than most
But brittle-er than mud or sand it seemed.
Like hardened shells of eggs encased in cloth.

Yet several further forward steps he takes
And with the words that ring inside his ears
His eyes, as told, stay firmly fixed ahead.
Not once sneaking adrift to peer below.

But as he finds the centre of the field
An awful sound does start to prick his ears.

MUSIC – 'KILLING FIELDS' - sea of souls.

BERT stops, we hear the groans.

Like groans collective, seeping from the souls
Of lost folk, now awakened from cold sleep.
And with each step his boots do heavy grow
As ground below begins to snap and burst.
A sinking feeling rising in his chest
The old familiar stench crawls down his throat.

One final step he takes before he feels
A desperate grip that curls around his leg
The feel of human fingers clutching hold
The helpless plea of men been left for dead.

And nothing then could stop the instinct fierce
As eyes drop down to look below his feet.

MUSIC – 'KILLING FIELDS' – The soundscape stops and is replaced by birdsong

ANIMATION 5.   *We see a field projected around him – stationary.*

And suddenly he finds himself transported
To back inside a memory so raw.
He feels the air of France fill up his lungs
And brightness of the sky stings sharp his eyes.

He stands upon a field where once grew grass,
Now only bloodied limbs do pierce the mud.
And bony fingers clutching fruitless stand,
Like stalks whose flowers long have disappeared.

Bert fights to hold the bile in his guts
And grips his legs to try and keep his feet.
A place he thought he'd left behind for good
A scene of hell sits fresh to be relived.

He closes eyes and bites down on his lip.
Remembering the words the creature spat.

THE GUIDE appears through the gauze.

GUIDE   *'Your pace must never pass beyond a walk*
               No matter what the fear within your heart.'

BERT steps backwards on to the structure as the animation of the ground starts t
moves past him. The Killing Field comes alive. Hands and faces appear throug.
the structure, grabbing at BERT.

BERT (attached to a harness) continues to step backward until he is standin
horizontal on the centre panel of the Trench, creating a birdseye view of hir
crossing no man's land.

BERT	He wanders slowly, heavy boots all caked,
	And sodden as they break the earth below.
	Like virgin snow, it crunches under foot,
	As youth and dreams and loves are crushed beneath.
	He walks on, at a measured pace, his fear
	Paralysed underneath the weight of lead
	That fills the air, and noise that fills his head.
	On and on he walks, no end in sight.
	The sounds of air expelled from lungs surrounds,
	The smell of flesh, that bursts and burns confounds.
	The flecks of blood and brain and bone that land
	Upon his skin like snowflakes, hot with life
	That once was full of possibility
	but now just serves to fertilise the land.
	Too many ghosts to haunt this empty place.
	Bert breathes down to his boots and eyes ahead
	He ushers forth each straw of strength he has
	And step by step he finds the field's edge.

ANIMATION 5 *disappears, as do the hands and faces behind, as BERT steps off the structure. Peace, silence.*

	The moment that his feet do leave the mud.
	The screeching sound of horror disappears.
	And when he turns around to look behind
	Nothing but an empty field he sees.

'MAYFLOWERS' – GUIDE THEME

GUIDE	*'The first trial is complete'*
CHORUS 1	rings out a voice.
BERT	And Bert turns round to see the beast's black eyes.
GUIDE	*'The second lies in wait should you proceed.*
	But know that further horrors lurk ahead.'
BERT	Bert looks down at his hand to see it shake
	As hot adrenalin pipes through his veins.
	He catches breath and clenches weary fists.

Then forward steps, a steel within his heart.

GUIDE   *'Along this path a chamber you shall find.*
Wherein resides a strange and vivid beast.
Its riddle you must solve for you to pass.
But be sure to answer quick and answer true
For know within its breath a poison lies
Enough to send men mad and even worse.'

'SEPARATED BY A SMILE' – PART ONE

BERT moves deeper and deeper inside the tunnels, a large plank is rotated on his back to create an endless moving tunnel roof.

CHORUS 3   And with those words the creature holds his gaze
Then turns and shuffles into dark once more.

BERT   Bert grits his yellow teeth and presses on.
The dim and pitted path shows him the way.

'SEPARATED BY A SMILE' – HALF VERSE

BERT stoops to a crouch, the plank on his back.

Before too long the tunnel's walls constrict
And Bert is forced to crawl that he may pass.
He feels the solid clay beneath his hands,
The crumbling earth that scrapes atop his head.

The roots of trees long dead reach down to stroke
his back as if to see if he is real.
He drudges through these bow-els of the world
'till up ahead he spies a yellow glow.
And out he's poured into a hollowed room
Where there ahead his greeter lies in wait.

The plank is removed.

A huge puppet of THE DEMON is revealed, it looms over the stage, its head is like a terrifying distorted gas mask. The stage is filled with smoke.

The Demon's shape is hard to tell at first,
It seems to almost rise up from a mist.

A cloudy mustard hue its form doth take
And at the top a hard and fearsome face
That shakes Bert's nerve in cold and desp'rate fear.

Two empty eyes stare deep into his soul
like darkened portholes of a sunken ship.
And long and slender beak that stretches out
Like muz-zle of a horse but hard and sharp.
And through this trunk the wheezing sound of breath
Doth scrape like gravel poured upon a grate.

DEMON	*'You wish to pass?'*
BERT	the spectre hisses soft

and as he does Bert sees its breath expel
a dense mist that sits heavier than air.
Which creeps toward him sure and silently.
Bert looks down to his boots and notices,
The ground is slicked with oily residue.

He feels his skin begin to prick and burn
A sickness in his stomach starts to rise.
His eyes begin to itch and sting and swell
His throat feels raw, like stripped of all its flesh.

DEMON	*'If riddle you can solve you may proceed*
	But should you fail your grave be where you fall.'
BERT	And then the monster rose to its full height

And heaved its question from its poisoned lungs.

DEMON	*'What thing can sate a Warlord's appetite?*
	Or soothe a battle widow's broken heart?
	What can bring back the sons and daughters lost?
	Or makes the shed of blood seem justified?'
BERT	Bert feels the breath surround him like a fog,

His skin alight like fire, blister'd and cracked.
Metallic taste of blood crawls in his mouth
And ground feels like 'tis ripped from underneath.

He fixes on the words that sting his mind.
He pictures leaders mongering their wars.
The weeping wives when telegrams received
And parents losing that they held most dear.
He searches through all reason he might find
For end to justify these hateful means?

And in that moment he recalls his wife
And unborn baby cruelly ripped away.

He looks into the creature's deadened eyes
His hanging face, like a devil's sick of sin;
And suddenly the answer rings out clear.
And with his final ounce of breath he rasps:

'No thing can sate a Warlord's appetite
Or soothe a battle widow's broken heart.
No thing brings back the sons and daughters lost.
Or makes the shed of blood seem justified.
'Nothing. That's the answer that you seek.'

'SEPARATED BY A SMILE' – instrumental verse starts

And as those words escape Bert's crackened lips
The beast evaporates into the air
Its heavy skull drops empty at Bert's feet.
Leaving just a cloak of mist behind.

THE DEMON puppet disintegrates, leaving the mask on the floor.

With no breath left, Bert falls down to his knees
And pulls the creature's mask upon his face.
Then just like icy water from a spring
He swallows gulps of air and fills his lungs.
And through the windows of the creature's eyes
He finds his feet and passes through the fog.

He staggers further through the darkened lanes
His heart emboldened with each taken step.
His eyes adjusting to the lack of light
As if becoming part of this dark world.

'SEPARATED BY A SMILE' – CHORUS

The side flats are manipulated to create the final tunnel.

> The passage widens to a chambered hall
> With pillars grand, stretched down from ancient roots
> That twist and gnarl, like oaken limbs entwined
> The bodies of the Gods laid down to sleep.

The flats become a huge door.

> Set deep within the roots there lies a door.
> That looks though it had stood since dawn of time.
> And built either to keep unwanteds out
> Or p'raps to hold something far worse inside.
> Sitting high twixt the tangled webs of branch
> The cloven creature watches blankly on.

'MAYFLOWERS' – GUIDE THEME

GUIDE *'You've reached the final trial of your quest*
and with it comes the chance to prove your worth.
Beyond this door a Guardian awaits
Who holds within the key to set you free.
This demon you must conquer to proceed
or else be trapped in dark forever more.'

BERT And as he speaks the cumbrous door unlocks
And with the hoary creak of ancient wood,
it open creeps upon its hefty hinge
revealing forth the path for Bert to take.

The door opens. BERT walks through.

> Bert summons all the stocks retained within
> And presses forth once more upon his quest.
> With leaden foot he trudges through the gloom
> To hear the heavy door slam hard behind
> And trap him with whatever lays within.

*The doors close on BERT, to then re-open almost instantly but now revealing
the scene of a working trench, full of soldiers - created by the CHORUS.*

A few more careful steps he takes inside
And as his eyes adjust to the dim light
He recognises that in which he stands
And deep remembered fears grab swift ahold.

He finds himself stood in familiar trench
like that in which he'd lived for countless days.

The filthy, rutted duck-boards under foot
and sodden sandbags stacked against the mud.
The signs of soldiers littering the way.
A stench of death and excrement abides.
The pools of sludge all mixed with rum and blood,
Old boots, and rats and relics of those lost.
Endless wire, like barbed and bloody bunting
To celebrate the horrors all around.

Stood lurking in the dark of this foxhole.
Face obscured beneath its heavy helmet.
A figure hunches, fearsome in its sight.
Drenched in steely grey of En'my garb.

One of the CHORUS holds an enemy helmet, with two glowing eyes to represent the figure.

Throughout the following section each member of the CHORUS has two enemy helmets, they are all used to create the effect of this helmeted creature being able to move around the space at great speed and also to change its shape at will.

It turns to Bert, then without any thought
It lunges t'ward him, rabid in its pace.
Bert's instincts pull his hand towards his hip
But weapon was long lost along the way.

Before he even has the chance to think
The figure smashes heavily upon
And thrusts Bert's body hard into the mud
With fever only capable from man
Who knows kill or be killed is all that stands.

The CHORUS surrounds him with their enemy helmets.

The du-el that doth follow hath no grace
There's no heroic ballet to behold.
Just feral, desp'rate, creatures battle-ing
Not for honour or country, just their life.

The fight begins. The Enemy helmets manipulated to attack BERT from all directions.

BERT is physically attacked by unseen hands and feet.

The stamp of boot, the hammer of a fist
thump dull against the living bone and flesh.
Fingers tear and gouge and rip and claw
And tighten roughly round opponents' necks.

Faces are pushed beneath the sickly mud
And sticks and bricks and elbows utilized

Finally BERT manages to defeat his assailant, which turns back into a single man.

He beats the man into submission.

'Til fin'lly one man's will outlives his foe
And yet another light is doused with woe.

Bert's heart beats fast, his breath returns in waves
The blood that's on his hands is not his own.
No pride is there to take, nor victory
Just grudging continuity of breath.

BERT looks over to his opponent and moves toward him.

He looks to where his fierce opponent lies
The evil brute his King taught him to hate
And reaching down pulls helmet from his head
To see the fearsome face that lies beneath.

But in the visage staring back at him
the features that he sees are of his own.
The youth that he once was lays at his feet
the fickle flame of life now fading fast.

Bert barely recognises in his eyes
The child that once existed in its place.
And all that he can do is hold him close
And comfort him as death's cold rattle shakes.

BERT holds the dying soldier in his hands.

'SEPARATED BY A SMILE' – instrumental verse begins

Tears come not, just emptiness resounds
Another penny falling in the drum.
There are no sobs within with which to grieve
No curses left to shriek into the sky.

'SEPARATED BY A SMILE'– song builds over the following to merge with the explosion theme from 'WEIGHT OF THE WORLD'

We watch the SOLDIER turn into a dragon

But as Bert holds the broken body close
He feels its flesh surrounding start to shake.
The uniform begins to stretch and tear
as bones beneath begin to change their shape.
Bert takes a step away, his eyes awide
In disbelief at what he sees before

Where once was skin now scales start to form
hard bony ridges piercing through its hide.
Where fingernails should be now claws emerge
And grows a tail, like serpent from the sea.
The face, no longer recognised as man
Shows snout and teeth and snarling, smoking breath
And fin'lly bursting from the creatures back
Two giant wings stretch forth like Angel's limbs.

The dragon turns to fix Bert with a stare
and like volcano spits forth floods of fire.
Then with a roar that shakes the ground below
It flaps its giant wings with all its might
And smashes through the earth over their heads
To burst forth to the heavens far above.

'SEPARATED BY A SMILE' – builds to a crescendo.

The dragon swoops across the stage and bursts through the centre panel of the Trench.

A bright light pours through the hole.

> Bert stands below the newly opened hole
> And feels a light shine down upon his face.

A hand bursts through and grabs BERT.

> Then suddenly feels grip upon his arm
> And sound of creatures from another time.

A SOLDIER appears through the breach.

SOLDIER	*'Is that you Bert?'*
BERT	Cries down familiar voice
SOLDIER	*'We're here to get you out, just take my hand,* *we have to hurry cos this hole won't last* *But just one final push and you'll be free.'*
BERT	A hope stirs in Bert's soul he'd thought was lost And suddenly the urge to live burns bright. But as he tries to start his sweet ascent A noise rings faintly from the dark below. He turns his head and strains his ears to hear And sure enough there comes a baby's cry. Then letting go of saviour's hand above Bert turns and disappears back to the gloom.
SOLDIER	*'Bert!'*
BERT	comes the cry that issues from above
SOLDIER	*'The tunnel will not hold, we have to go!'*
BERT	But Bert ignores the warnings in his ears and runs towards the infant's weeping wail, until he finds a collapsed wooden beam and body trapped and bleeding underneath.

> *'My son'* he cries as tears prick at his eyes
> and then with every ounce of strength he owns
> he grips the wood and lifts with all his worth
> And there below lies Collins still alive.

BERT moves the debris to reveal the body of COLLINS beneath the Trench structure.

> He grabs the boy and drags him through the mud
> Whilst praying that he will not be too late.
> 'Til up ahead he spies the divine light
> and hears the voices calling through the breach.

SOLDIER *'The tunnel's closing there's no time to spare*
the earth's collapsing even as we speak.'

BERT lifts COLLINS into the air; he takes the hand of the SOLDIER that reaches through the structure.

> Then Bert takes Collins tightly in his arms
> And lifts his dear friend high above his head.
> to pass him up into the waiting hands
> and see him disappear into the light.

The centre panel then lowers as COLLINS passes through it.

Behind we reveal the rescuers above, they pull COLLINS up out of the tunnel.

SOLDIER 2 The men pull Collins up into their arms.
as tunnel falls and crumbles all around.

SOLDIER And as the boy emerges from the hole
The earth gives birth to yet another son.

COLLINS Yet as is wont, with life must follow death
And Bert is swallowed by the dark anew.

The panel is then pulled back up to reveal BERT alone beneath.

> He sits below in blackness once again
> And feels the stale air round him start to thin.
> He shuts his eyes and leans against the mud,

His body weak, his breath begins to slow.
And as he, weary, submits to the end.
A gentle smile flickers 'cross his face.

Pause.

'MAYFLOWERS' – GUIDE THEME

GUIDE   *'You passed the final test'*

CHORUS 3   calls out a voice

CHORUS 1   And from the dark steps his unearthly guide

GUIDE   *'You've shown the strength of heart which you possess*
                 and proved you're worthy of that which you seek
                 You willing, gave the price that you were asked.
                 Now time has come for you to claim your prize.'

CHORUS 3   The creature nods then turns upon its heel
                 And with one final look…

CHORUS 1   …he disappears.

MUSIC – 'INTO THE DEEP'

BERT looks out and slowly a light starts to build on his face. It grows and grows in intensity.

Then from the black a glow begins to swell
and figure dressed in white starts to emerge.
Bert rubs his salty eyes and takes a breath
As with each step the angel grows more clear.
'Til soon before him stands his darling wife.
And in her arms a beaut'ful babe doth sleep.

'INTO THE DEEP' – interspersed with verse

She puts her hand upon Bert's trembling cheek
And whispers tender words into his ear.

Bert looks down to the infant in her arms
And feels his heart swell deep within his chest.

Then with one perfect kiss she takes his hand
And leads him gently t'ward the brilliant light.

Instrumental chorus.

> And with each step Bert takes, a weight doth lift
> As ling'ring fear begins to loose its grip.
> The smell of death starts fading from his lungs
> The sight of blood clean washes from his eyes
> The cry of bombs and guns begin to cease
> And fin'lly Bert lets go, at last at peace.

The light builds until the music kicks in and it fills the stage.

After a few moments it drops to blackout and the remainder of the song plays over the curtain call.

The End.

OTHER OLIVER LANSLEY TITLES

Holly and Ivan's Christmas Adventure
9781849431361

Flies
9781849432146

The Infant
9781849432283

Oliver Lansley: Les Enfants Terribles; Collected Plays
The Terrible Infants / Ernest And The Pale Moon /
The Vaudevillains
9781849431637

WWW.OBERONBOOKS.COM

Follow us on www.twitter.com/@oberonbooks
& www.facebook.com/oberonbook